Pebble®
Plus

Earth and Space Science

Forecasting Weather

by Terri Sievert

CAPSTONE PRESS
a capstone imprint

Pebble Plus is published by Capstone Press,
1710 Roe Crest Drive, North Mankato, Minnesota 56003.
www.capstonepub.com

Books published by Capstone Press are manufactured with paper
containing at least 10 percent post-consumer waste.

Library of Congress Cataloging-in-Publication Data
Sievert, Terri.
  Forecasting weather / by Terri Sievert.
    p. cm. — (Pebble plus. Earth and space science)
  Includes bibliographical references and index.
  Summary: "Simple text and full-color photos explain the science behind forecasting the weather"—Provided by
publisher.
  ISBN 978-1-4296-6813-2 (library binding) — ISBN 978-1-4296-7141-5 (paperback)
  1. Weather forecasting—Juvenile literature. I. Title. II. Series.
  QC995.43.S542 2012
  551.63—dc22   2011005135

Editorial Credits
Gillia Olson, editor; Lori Bye, designer; Wanda Winch, media researcher; Laura Manthe, production specialist

Photo Credits
Alamy: Ryan McGinnis, 19; Capstone, 12, 15; Capstone Studio: Karon Dubke, 7, 21 (all); Dreamstime: Ron Chapple
Studios, 5; NASA, 11; NOAA, 17; Shutterstock: Carolina K. Smith, M.D., cover, Oksana Perkins, 9, Robert Fesus, 1;
SuperStock Inc.: Flirt, 13

Note to Parents and Teachers

The Earth and Space Science series supports national science standards related to earth and
space science. This book describes and illustrates weather forecasting. The images support early
readers in understanding the text. The repetition of words and phrases helps early readers learn
new words. This book also introduces early readers to subject-specific vocabulary words, which
are defined in the Glossary section. Early readers may need assistance to read some words and to
use the Table of Contents, Glossary, Read More, Internet Sites, and Index sections of the book.

Printed in the United States of America in North Mankato, Minnesota.
112012   007045R

Table of Contents

Forecasts

What should you wear today?

Will it rain on the picnic?

Every day, scientists say what

the coming weather could be.

They make a weather forecast.

Meteorologists

Meteorologists are scientists

who forecast the weather.

They gather information

about past and present weather.

Then they make a forecast.

TOMORROW

Sunny Skies

Highs:85-90

Winds: NE 10-15

Climate

Weather is what is happening right now. Climate is the usual weather in a place over time. We study climate to help us know what the weather will be.

9

Air Masses

Air collects in huge chunks
called air masses.

Air masses move around Earth.

As warm masses rise above
cold masses, wind is created.

The leading edge of an air mass is called a front. Moving fronts usually bring weather changes. Weather maps often show fronts as lines.

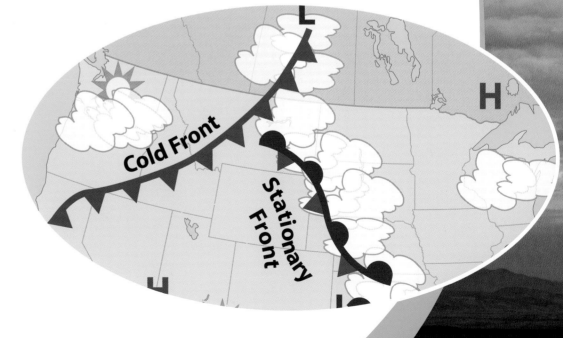

Air Pressure

Changes in air pressure can affect weather. Falling air pressure may bring rain or snow. Rising air pressure may mean fair weather.

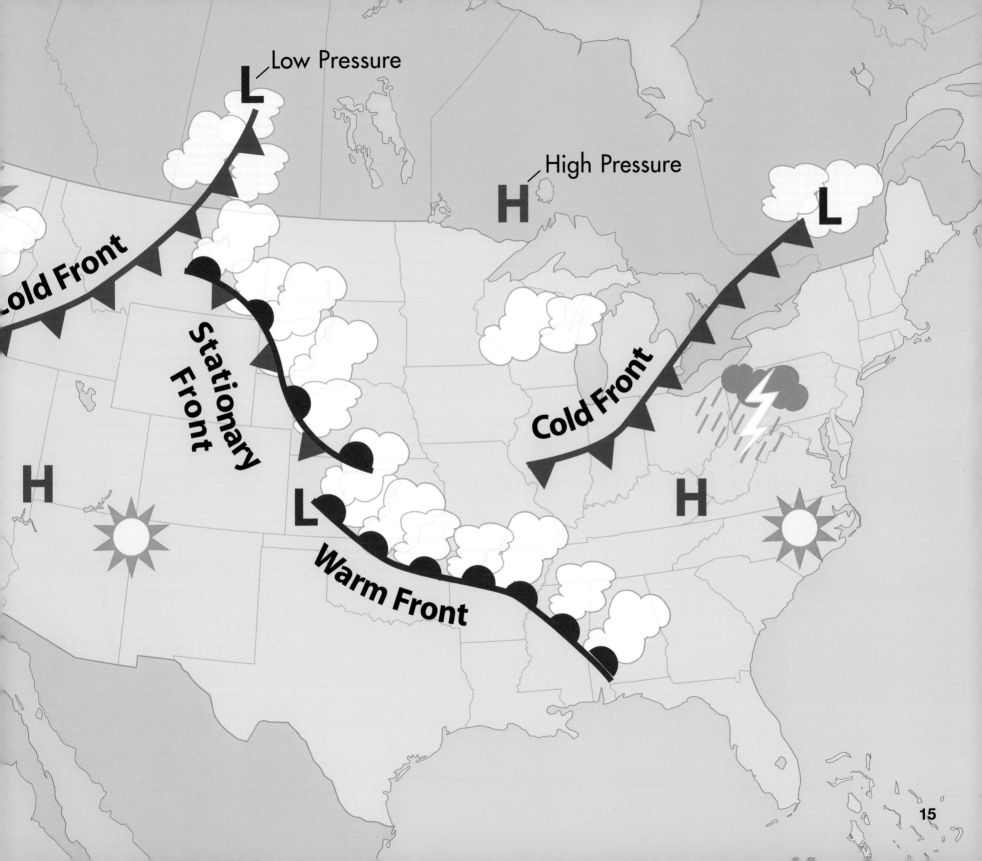

Low Pressure

L

High Pressure

H

L

Cold Front

Stationary Front

Cold Front

H

L

Warm Front

H

Satellites

Satellites circle Earth.

They take pictures that show clouds and storms.

Scientists watch how a storm moves to see where it's going.

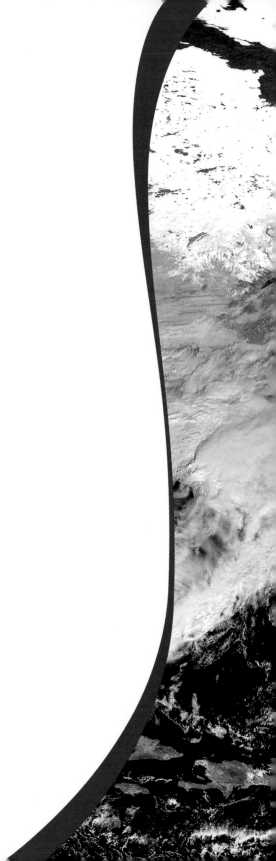

Radar

Radar waves sent through the
air bounce off rain and snow.
Radar pictures show how much
rain or snow is in clouds.
It also shows a storm's speed.

Make a Rain Gauge

A rain gauge measures rainfall. You can make one and record how much rain falls in a month.

You will need:
- clear cup or glass
- plastic ruler
- tape
- calendar
- pencil

1. Tape the ruler to the clear cup so that the zero end starts at the bottom of the cup. Set the cup outside in a spot where it can catch rain.
2. Every day, measure how much rain fell. Dump out the cup after each measurement.
3. Record the measurements on the calendar each day for a month. At the end of the month, add up all the rain. How much do you think it will rain next year during that month?

Glossary

air mass—a huge chunk of air that has the same temperature and amount of moisture

air pressure—the weight of air on a surface

climate—the usual weather in a place over time

fair—not stormy

radar—an instrument that can find raindrops or snowflakes by sending out microwaves

satellite—a machine that circles Earth; satellites are often used to gather weather information

Read More

Birch, Robin. *Watching Weather.* Weather and Climate. New York: Marshall Cavendish Benchmark, 2009.

Hanson, Anders. *Meteorologist's Tools.* Professional Tools. Edina, Minn.: ABDO Pub., 2011.

Slade, Suzanne. *How Do Tornadoes Form?: And Other Questions Kids Have about Weather.* Kids' Questions. Mankato, Minn.: Picture Window Books, 2010.

Internet Sites

FactHound offers a safe, fun way to find Internet sites related to this book. All of the sites on FactHound have been researched by our staff.

Here's all you do:

Visit *www.facthound.com*

Type in this code: 9781429668132

Check out projects, games and lots more at
www.capstonekids.com

Index

Word Count: 194
Grade: 1
Early-Intervention Level: 22